CLASSICAL GUITAR
Christmas Sheet Music

30 Holiday Favorites
Arranged for Solo Classical Guitar

ARRANGED BY JOHN HILL

ISBN 978-1-4950-2586-0

HAL•LEONARD®
CORPORATION
7777 W. BLUEMOUND RD. P.O. BOX 13819 MILWAUKEE, WI 53213

In Australia Contact:
Hal Leonard Australia Pty. Ltd.
4 Lentara Court
Cheltenham, 3192 Victoria, Australia
Email: ausadmin@halleonard.com.au

Visit Hal Leonard Online at
www.halleonard.com

Angels We Have Heard on High

Traditional French Carol
Translated by James Chadwick

As with Gladness Men of Old

Words by William Chatterton Dix
Music by Conrad Kocher

Tuning:
(low to high) D-A-D-G-B-E

Brightly

Auld Lang Syne

Tuning:
(low to high) D-A-D-G-B-E

Words by Robert Burns
Traditional Scottish Melody

Away in a Manger

Words by John T. McFarland (v.3)
Music by James R. Murray

Christ Was Born on Christmas Day

Traditional

Coventry Carol

Words by Robert Croo
Traditional English Melody

Deck the Hall

Traditional Welsh Carol

The First Noel

17th Century English Carol
Music from W. Sandys' Christmas Carols

Go, Tell It on the Mountain

Tuning:
(low to high) D-A-D-G-B-E

African-American Spiritual
Verses by John W. Work, Jr.

God Rest Ye Merry, Gentlemen

19th Century English Carol

Good King Wenceslas

Words by John M. Neale
Music from Piae Cantiones

Hallelujah Chorus

from MESSIAH

By George Frideric Handel

Hark! The Herald Angels Sing

Words by Charles Wesley
Altered by George Whitefield
Music by Felix Mendelssohn-Bartholdy
Arranged by William H. Cummings

Here We Come A-Wassailing

Traditional

The Holly and the Ivy

18th Century English Carol

I Saw Three Ships

Traditional English Carol

Tuning:
(low to high) D-A-D-G-B-E

Jingle Bells

Tuning:
(low to high) D-A-D-G-B-E

Words and Music by J. Pierpont

Jolly Old St. Nicholas

Traditional 19th Century American Carol

Joy to the World

Words by Isaac Watts
Music by George Frideric Handel
Adapted by Lowell Mason

20

March
from THE NUTCRACKER

By Pyotr Il'yich Tchaikovsky

O Christmas Tree

Traditional German Carol

Tuning:
(low to high) D-A-D-G-B-E

Moderately

O Come, All Ye Faithful
(Adeste Fideles)

Music by John Francis Wade
Latin Words translated by Frederick Oakeley

O Holy Night

French Words by Placide Cappeau
English Words by John S. Dwight
Music by Adolphe Adam

O Little Town of Bethlehem

Words by Phillips Brooks
Music by Lewis H. Redner

Silent Night

Words by Joseph Mohr
Translated by John F. Young
Music by Franz X. Gruber

Tuning:
(low to high) D-A-D-G-B-E

Moderately

The Twelve Days of Christmas

Traditional English Carol

Up on the Housetop

Words and Music by B.R. Hanby

We Three Kings of Orient Are

Words and Music by John H. Hopkins, Jr.

We Wish You a Merry Christmas

Traditional English Folksong

What Child Is This?

Words by William C. Dix
16th Century English Melody